THE DEMOCRAT BLUE WAVE IS THE ZOMBIE APOCALYPSE

Our Rights and Freedoms are Threatened by Mob Rule and the Rise of Socialism

T. H. Logwood

"We are a nation of laws... only if they are upheld"

ZOMBIES ARE REAL

Only Hollywood can make monsters come to life, and the zombie craze is no different. In a plethora of films, from Dawn of the Dead, to Z Nation, and the Walking Dead series, the undead are the dread, and the source of countless nightmares. The horror is fantasy for sure, but in a realistic sense, the behaviors of the "radical left wing" (Progressives) of the democratic party do portray a zombie-like state.

It is the control of the masses, not just from the radical left of the democrats, but this is true of any political party. Control being, by speech, thought, actions, or ideologies, that aligns under those of a group of elites seeking to dictate every facet of our lives.

This is known as Zombieism. The masses become a zombie-like puppet of the elitists and power brokers to do their will, in an almost mindless deadened state. These Zombie Masters have brainwashed an entire generation to believe that if they are elected to power, they will provide for their needs. The socialist ideology is becoming the foundation of the party, with its ranks swelling like a virus. It is not only frightening, but also happening, especially as the next round of politicians seeks election.

The bottom line is, that Zombieism spells the end of individual rights, freedoms, and liberties, contrary to the rule of law, and those guaranteed under the U.S. Constitution. If the radical wing is allowed to spread its blue wave of socialist ideology across the country, then America as we know it will be lost. It would be a nightmare come true.

ZOMBIES AND ZOMBIEISM

What is a zombie, and what is Zombieism all about? Basically, it is control. Control of thought by something else, by someone else, or from groups in power. It is a mass hysteria that defies logic and reason, fairness, and perhaps the rule of law. An ideology essentially that turns normal reasonable people into the hideous monsters as portrayed in every horror film. In other words, it's socialism, the few in power controlling the masses which become a mindless collective.

Not that ideologies are always a bad thing, or the mass belief in something, even inspired by charismatic leaders. No, not to misunderstand the point. When reason and fairness, and the rule of law, is given over to mob-violence, mass lunacy, insanity among the masses, then something is wrong. When there are issues effecting us all, can we not sit down together and discuss them in rational debates to find mutually beneficial solutions?

Or, does mob-rule, urged on by those few in authority, turn an issue into mass delusion, causing irrational behavior on a massive level, negatively effecting society as a whole? When is it alright to flip the ideas and beliefs that we grew up with, once viewed as "good", now is called "bad"? And then to indoctrinate masses of people to believe it and follow suite. When is having traditionally accepted "wrongs", suddenly becoming "right"? In almost an instant, by the spreading of some sort of contagious disease or virus, many of our precepts and ideas are turned topsy-turvy. It is this sudden mass change of counter-ideologies that Zombieism is all about. We have witnessed those changes in every facet of our society. It is the "cancel-culture" or "political correctness" craze that suppresses free and open speech, debate versus hate speech. It seems to be the whole idea of "it's our way, or we will send the zombie masses to intimidate you".

Some of these notions include: the police are bad, open borders is fairness, firearms are evil, destroying statues and defaming national heroes, being energy independent as "racist", our Founding Fathers were "white supremacists", gender dysphoria, removing "Christ" from Christmas and Christmas songs, the murder of babies (abortion) as acceptable, and government control of our lives (socialism) as desirable. And then to try and reason and offer factual informational, the

Like in every zombie movie, life is normal and going along fine. Then suddenly it seems that some people are getting sick or weird, by some strange behavior. And then they become changed, not in a good way, but in a violent destructive manner, which then spreads to the masses like a virus. The masses spread destruction and death, then towards the end of the film, civility is restored (but not in all cases).

What are we facing today in our country, as we seem ever divided and pitted against each other, is an insane and irrational meltdown of civility promoted by various groups, leaders, and politicians. Do we let the zombies take over, or can we band together to restore some common normalcy?

THE HATE TRUMP
MOVEMENT

One of the great things this country offers, is the election cycle. By constitutional law, this country is to have free and fair elections, whereby the governed will periodically elect its leaders from their peers. And for the most part, for over 200 years, our system of elections and voting has been fairly honest. The outcomes are sometimes a question, but when one side loses, they lick their wounds, get on with business, and plan for the next election. At least, that is how it should be.

For example, the 2016 presidential election turned a new chapter is Zombieism. One might characterize the entire election period as an unending barrage of hate-speech, threats, temper-tantrums, zombie protests, and a bias inflammatory media spreading yellow journalism the likes of which parallels Nazi Germany. The democrats could not stand the fact, literally the fact, that Donald J. Trump was elected president, over their criminally deceptive failure of a Zombieist in Ms. Clinton.

Who is Donald J. Trump anyways? He is an outsider, businessman, real estate tycoon, playboy, TV star, republican, moderate conservative, a disruptor of the status quo, and a nationalist. Who in their right mind would have ever guessed that "he" would become president, leader of the free world, defender of the Constitution, and for now bringer to a halt of the zombie apocalypse. Against all odds, he won, and the leftist zombie party of democrat stooges has not accepted this reality, to this very point. And they never will.

Not only the democrats, but the republican "rhinos" and "never-Trumpers", the entrenched swamp rats of the DC power cesspool, all have been against him ever since his announcement to run for president. It isn't just a dislike for the president, but a hatred as for everything that he is and stands for. These are the Zombie Masters, those seeking to control the masses with their own sick propaganda of one worldism and global control. They have been seeking power and control for decades now, with the aim of destroying the constitution and all of the freedoms granted therein.

Even in the political volleying today, over the border wall and security, the Zombieists Nancy Pelosi (House Majority Leader) and Chuck Schumer (Senate Minority Leader) have shown what's in their hearts, hatred. They have a hatred towards the president, hatred of the constitution, hatred of truth and fairness, and hatred of the free people that side with the president. If politics and the control of the masses is more important than doing what is right and best for the nation, then those types of leaders need to be voted out of office. Are these leaders serving the people of this country, as they swore to do, or are they serving their own ends, at the expense of us all?

President Trump is not the issue per se. It's what he has done, and what he hopes to accomplish that the Trump-Haters oppose. Those things are upholding the Constitution and the rule of law, enforcing the laws and due process, reducing government control in our lives, the right-to-life, and preserving our rights and liberties. In a society where government holds all of the power and makes decisions on behalf of the people, free speech is not tolerated, the Good for the people is marginalized, and the health and productivity of the nation is stifled. "Power held in the hands of a few, will bring ruin to a nation."

WIN AT ALL COST

"The only way Democrats can win, is to cheat". Manipulation and deceit, with the backing of main stream media, and powerful wealthy donors, the democrats are using Gestapo-like tactics to quell any resistance, twist truths and news, and use the "mob" (or horde) of zombies to intimidate and harass opposition. Look at the antics they pulled during the 2016 and 2018 elections. Aren't they are doing the same in 2020?

This is not the democratic party of JFK or even Bill Clinton. What was the welfare of the working man under the Kennedy-era Democrats, which was the cornerstone of the party, has given way to a radical socialistic dogma, with legions of brain-washed stooges (zombies) to carry out mob violence and sow endless discord. Rather than come up with solutions to fix an issue, or make lives better for the people, they use rhetoric and hate speech, and the double-standard, to advance a dark agenda. Is this what democrats want from their party and the party stewardship?

Voter fraud and identity theft are on a national scale, according to many experts. This is one area where the democrats have opened up their bag of dirty tricks. During the numerous democrat voter registration drives, many of the registration cards will ask for birth date, address, and last four numbers of the social security number. That is sensitive personal information that is never anyone's business to know. Why is that needed?

As the Springfield, Missouri democratic office would reply, "that information is used for follow-up purposes". The scary prospect is that the personal information is being sold or used, to make fake voter registrations. And it does happen, and far too frequently according to various news stories. Personal information is an identity theft resource, that can (and has been documented) be used to fill voter registration boxes and vote tallies. If this is in fact true, and done in other places, then fake people can be set up as voters all across the country. And with little to no verification, fraud, in the worst possible way can occur.

Let's not forget the masses of "ballots" that suddenly appear after the vote tallies are completed, like in Palm Beach County, Florida, in Atlanta, Georgia, and in Arizona (just to cite a few). Were these real and honest votes, or "just in time" to sway the election results? That never happens to benefit republican candidates.

Remember the "hanging chads" in Florida? It was the 2004 Presidential race between George Bush and Al Gore, where the Florida electoral vote might had gone to Gore if the "chads" were favorable. The particular ballot used a card punch system, whereby the vote cast was made using a pin or punch through the paper ballot. Sometimes the punches were only partially made, others had more than one punch (such s a change in vote), but this created a huge controversy. For months, ballot recounts and debates on how votes were cast, went on and on. Fake ballots and manipulated ballots appeared to further add confusion. The majority of these ballots were from the southern democrat controlled counties.

At least four of the nationally covered races from the 2018 midterm elections, were highly contested by the democrats, resulting in one race over turned by suspicious means. Once the voting is over, within the time period allowed by law, that is the end, is it not? No, apparently not. But wait... "surprise, surprise, surprise", to quote Gomer Pyle from the famous TV show, when magically, thousands of untallied ballots miraculously appeared "after" the final vote count. And surprisingly, "All" of these mysterious ballots were marked for the democrat candidate. In all of these cases, the "misplaced" ballots were 100% for the democratic party candidate. How is that possible? That would be a statistical impossibility! Hmm, highly suspicious, and there was no way they were real. The only way democrats can win is to cheat? Shameful! JFK, where are you?

In four 2018 highly reported races, those for the governorships in Georgia and Florida, and for the senator seat in Texas and Arizona, the results were very close and won by the republican candidates. The democrats objected and contested them. This has happened now for several years, in almost every race where the republican candidate had won by a very small margin, the "miracle ballots" would magically appear. These new votes, have, or would have, pushed the other candidate over the top. This is fraud in the worst case.

In Arizona, signatures were not matching what was on record. Missing ballots suddenly appeared out of "manna", and the rightful republican winner of the race had then suddenly lost. A recount produced the ever-slightest victory for the democrat contender. This is no less a travesty to every ideal we hold as fair and impartial elections. This is yet another example of why voter ID laws can help stem the mischief.

In Broward County, Florida, Supervisor of Elections, Brenda Snipes, was again at the middle of the latest controversy. Suddenly after the election, when the democrat candidate lost the governors race, she (they) found thousands of missing ballots, all of which were marked for the democrat contender. The supervisor is to report results within 30 minutes after the polls close, and over 43 hours later, Broward and Palm Beach counties have not reported their legal results.

In fact, and reported on many news reports, a legal expert was brought in to contest the election result for governor. As the race was very close, the democrats again sought to change the outcome. It was reported this lawyer touted that, "the election result will be turned". And from there a legal fight and vote recount got underway. "They" claimed they found some hundreds of thousands of unsubmitted ballots just within the that single Florida county. No other county in the state has had so much controversy or "miracle ballots". This has happened several times over the past elections. If one were to do the math, that number of missing ballots, not only would have turned the governors race, but the added ballot count was far in excess of the number of voters registered on file in that county. This deceit is fraud of the worst kind, illegal in every sense of the laws we are suppose to be governed by. And yet, there was no investigation or prosecution of the wrongdoers. The rightful candidate for governor still won, but the democrats, under the leadership of Ms. Snipes in this case, tried every knavery to sway the election.

In earlier campaigns, 2000, she was accused of this same trick, controversy, of destroying ballots, missing ballots, and not removing ineligible voters from the records. And not to forget the 2004 presidential race, where the "hanging chads" volleyed the question of whom the intentions of the vote was for. This debacle also centered in Broward County.

These are crimes against everything this country was founded upon, and crimes that were not investigated. It's all very fishy, and grossly dishonest. How is it that we allow these people to run elections, run our governing offices, and are given control over our lives?

Without fair and reasonable voter ID laws, elections can then be swayed, and illegitimate candidates will have subverted our right to vote in our otherwise fair and free election system. "Fair and free", that is the premise and foundation of the laws for this country. Different than for all other nations, even throughout history, the hope for elections that are not tampered with, to freely choose the candidates, and then privately make their vote, has been the greatest liberty America offers. Is that freedom slipping away?

BEWARE THE
RED SHIRTS AND
BLUE HATS

One of the moves of the socialists has been to change or erase history, the history that is supposedly taught to our children. The school system and colleges, once proud institutions of learning, are degrading into the brown-shirt Hitler Youth-like training grounds. First, change the history to a more tolerant or different reality. If students are not taught history, history has a nasty way of being repeated. Next, brain washing, through various means, have produced many "red-shirts", now on the college campuses, shouting down opposing viewpoints, marching in violent protests, using laws and rules to suppress ideas contrary to their headmasters. And then, with young minds indoctrinated with socialistic principles, get them out to vote (democrat). Vote for the leaders that will mutate this country into the "Socialist States of Amerika", and all liberty will be lost.

Remember the red shirts? Has the history of Cambodia and the Paul Pott regime also been erased from the books? Our youth are becoming the Red Shirts of the new democrat socialist party. The youth have been trained to embrace many ideals and teachings that "we as kids" were told as evil for a free society. As the Paul Pott leaders gained in power, they used the brainwashed youth, the Cambodian zombies, to march in violent protest to squash free thought and opposition. They wore red shirts, burned books and destroyed property, pulled opposition people from their homes, then beat (or killed) them. They were the mobs that helped Pott destroy an otherwise open society. They killed how many millions of their own citizens? Never forget that, it is starting here.

The UN peacekeepers wear a sky blue colored hat while on occupation duty in various war-torn areas. The UN is run by a leader and a few high-ranking inner circle of people. Power is concentrated to the few, yet they hold authority over many nations in various laws and treaties. It has been said by some reporters, that if peace was not restored, like in a violent march or strike, then the UN could bring in peacekeepers to regain order.

Currently, that can not happen here, but that can change. Having foreign troops as an armed police force, on American soil, is a gross violation of our national sovereignty and rights. Yet, the zombie masters look forward to those days. where authority will be concentrated in the hands of a few, and they will determine what is can be done. But Blue Hats on our soil? Sure, it can happen, it was threatened once during the Obama/Biden years, according to one source. Now under what scenario might mercenary aide be needed here? Could a widespread crisis trigger a plea to the UN for help? How about to quell the violent zombie mobs in the cities as police departments are eliminated.

Many people in the public arena scream out about the Nazis. "Trump is a Nazi, fascist", is often played over the news programs to electrify the zombie masses. If the truths of history are no longer being taught in our schools as they really happened, then it makes sense that the public only knows a few catch phrases.

Find an older history book, or do the research, and learn about the national-socialist movement of the 1930's period in Germany. What events brought about the rise of the movement, and the leaders it produced? The Nazis suppressed free speech, squashed open expression from opposition, lied, cheated, murdered their opponents, used the media to twist and distort the truth, and indoctrinated the children in brain-washing schools with the ideas of "State-first" thinking. If what is happening today in our schools, on the streets where these zombie marches are happening, and through the twisted media, have any parallel to the past, then we as a free nation are in trouble. The new democrat party sure acts like the National Socialists of old, not like the defamed president or the republican party. Do we as a nation really want to venture down this road? It did not work out very well for the German people or the world.

Remember what Machiavelli warned back around 1500, "Power corrupts, and absolute power corrupts absolutely". And examining history, even recent history, this is exactly true. When leaders get into power, unchecked by laws and constitutional limitations, then the mischief that resides in a mans' heart, festers into evil. It is said that if a government is allowed to gain power (unchecked), then those leaders first abuse the power to their own gain. Then they oppress the people and silence opposition. And then, by historical fact, they mass murder their own citizens. Is not the legalized murder of unborn babies the same as mass murder? Perhaps a slightly different context, but the legalized killing of a nation's own citizens is unsettling.

Are we at that point in the history of our nation, that the killing of the most innocent and defenseless of citizens (unborn babies) is not only legal, but celebrated with glee by filthy politicians and bloodthirsty organizations? Who will be next? Children discarded by zombie-influenced parents? Then who, the elderly, Christians, the deplorable republicans, and where does it end? This country is on a dangerous slippery slope that has a firey bottom.

THE SOCIAL SECURITY SCAM

Another great worry over zombieist control relates to our earned wages. Control the masses via the paycheck, and keep raising taxes. Then take parts of the paycheck to fund various agendas. The Social Security system, meant for our good, is a lie. There are state and federal laws against individuals and companies that dupe people out of their hard-working money by pyramid schemes and deceptive financial-gain dealings. But when it comes to the federal government that initiates such schemes, it isn't called fraud, it's called a government program. And every program the government runs, just needs more (and more) money. But fraud is fraud, and it is still illegal (or should be).

The social security system has become a scam of another government control program, run by the "Zombie Masters", aided by corrupt politicians from both parties. Zombieism is mindless control of the masses, and in many respects, the social "insecurity" system is a mandated redistribution scheme of your hard-earned wages. It is not voluntary, and to object against such unconstitutional imposition, incurs heavy governmental wrath. And what is a social "good", is really a socialist ideal in practice.

In the 1930's when America was going through the worst depression ever, then President Roosevelt signed and approved the Social Security Act. The plan was to provide a "safety net" for employees, providing money at retirement so that particular worker would be able to have something in order to buy food, clothing, and housing, the basics. Each employee would be taxed a percentage of their wages, the income they worked to earn, and those funds would be set aside for that person upon retirement, with interest. On paper, that almost sounds reasonable and plausible. The truth is, as evidenced today, it is a socialist program of stealing from the worker, to redistribute income among the masses.

Socialism is government control. On the federal level, any time the government dictates who, how, and what, over our lives, it is socialism. Anything the government runs, or evens touches, becomes a boon-doggle disaster. Anytime the government decides where you will do something, how you will do a thing, what you are going to receive or pay, how much and how often, and so on, it is socialism. Certainly, in regards to your hard-earned wages, someone else, someone in authority knows better than you how to spend it. They do, and they have. Now on the state and local levels, governmental prowess is different. We are a system of rules and laws to help us, the governed, have a safe, peaceful, reasonably happy life. The laws define the limits of what we can do as to not interfere with the rights of others. That is the rule of law, as intended by our founding fathers, that fought for and designed the US Constitution. Over and beyond that, the feds overstep their bounds of control (laws), dictating the limits on our personal liberties.

And what was a "fair and reasonable" retirement plan imposed on behalf of the worker, has morphed into a wealth redistribution plan for every person across the national boundaries. Citizen or not, nearly everybody seems to have entitlement to "your" retirement-planned wages, so "they" can live within the "safety net". Laws and programs have grown so huge, offering help and benefits to many people via various medical and assistance avenues, that there is no money left in the coffers. The social security system is horribly in debt. The design was for a percentage of your wages to be held for "your" personal use, under your own discretion, when you are no longer working. It is a sham and a disgrace that "your" money is being used for all of these other places.

The design is reasonable, but when government controls something, especially by a small number of people, or even one person, then it becomes inefficient, wasteful, and corrupt. What government touches, it ruins.

But the "new" social security system, from your paycheck, helps with medical bills, children programs, financial aide to families, TV shows for underage kids, illegal migrants seeking a better life, legal migrants needing help for a new start, kickbacks and bribes to politicians and power brokers. Your money goes to contributions for organizations and political parties, and who really knows what else. That was your retirement. From many news stories, experts, and politicians, we hear how the system is deeply in debt, basically insolvent, with no easy way to make it work. Social security accounts for 59% of the federal budget (your tax dollars). Yes, obviously you can't make a system work if the funds are spent a hundred-fold. If our checkbooks were so overdrawn and so deeply in arrears as this government program, we would be forced to file bankruptcy and be thrown in jail for the fraudulent use of the funds. But that is government, and they make the laws. Politicians are only accountable to the electorate, if the election process is fair, and only if people vote.

And the lawmakers, some of them, not all, are zombie masters. There are groups and some politicians looking either fix or do away with some of the social security system. As it is a very touchy and difficult topic, any action remains just as it is, talk.

THE LAST ELECTION

The 2020 Presidential election may well be the last free election we have in this country. Our liberties and rights are slipping away with every election cycle, and soon, our freedom of speech (expressed through our vote) may disappear. Once our ability to speak freely is gone, then all of our other rights will be silenced as well.

Strong words and a bold statement, but it may be very true as we watch and wrestle with the political and legal events as they lead up to election. Watching the Fall 2018 elections, the trend and precursor for the next cycle is clear. Rather, the trend is scary. Opinion surveys and many commentators suggest that socialism and socialistic ideals are acceptable, and even desirable, particularly with younger adults. If the next generation, our youth and young adults, are so swayed by the promises of "free stuff" and "the government will take care of you", then we are in grave danger indeed. Every politician makes promises, many are unfulfilled, but in the zombieist mindset, they are just words to gain office. Listen to what is said, and compare the rhetoric to what has actually been done. That should give a clue as the reality of their promises.

Remember the Fall 2018 mid-term election? What was at stake, and who showed up to vote? The clamoring and saber-rattling from both the republican and democratic sides, coupled with the endless blabbering dribble from the bias media, spelled out clearly the goals of the democrat party. The vote, and the preservation of this country's liberties was decided by the independent voters. But for how much longer? Elected leaders are to serve the citizenry, not their own agendas. How well have they done?

At stake, according to the pro-republican stance, was stability and legality. Under the strong leadership of President Trump, the economy has blossomed to an unfathomable growth rate around 4% (give or take a smidge) almost immediately after he took office. He kept his campaign promises of bringing at least one (now two) "Originalist" supreme court justices to the bench, repealed burdensome and ridiculous government regulations, restored the rule of law (especially with regards to immigration), prevented disastrous world conflicts like with North Korea, among many other bold actions. The republican platform was to keep moving in this direction, build on job growth and the economy, following the "rule of law", fix the illegal alien and immigration mess, and restore civility among our divided peoples.

Now without question, the most active and vocal side of the democrat party clearly fought for the opposite platform. I say clearly, because there was never a single mention of policy, or what they would actually do to improve the lives of Americans. The left wing of the party took a different approach, and showed truly what the party stood for. The moderate and right wings of the democrat party remained ever still, perhaps turning into zombies themselves. Their intent was to unravel and destroy every positive action President Trump has accomplished. They yelled out hate-speech towards anything of growth, improvement, or prosperity. They shouted about impeaching the newly appointed justice to the supreme court. They writhed with hatred and threats of impeaching President Trump himself. They cried and had temper-tantrums about anything related to the mass invasion by illegal aliens. Never once, did any democrat candidate talk about "How" they would fix health care, restore jobs for Americans, do better with our international responsibilities, and so on. And to speak to the contrary, not fall in line with party thinking, they, and the media would "lamb-blast" you with emotional dribble and shouts or being a "racist".

Ok, if you are unhappy with a policy or action, tell us in clear unemotional manner of "what" you would do. Their entire political strategy was to slander and malign anyone and everything that was that contrary to their hate-filled dialogue. Even the mainstream media, heavily biased against the president, was in lock-step with the democrat zombie mob mentality. Emotionally driven trauma and drama, just like a pre-adolescent child.

AND WHO SHOWED
UP TO VOTE?

"It's that time again, elections." To some it's dread and bother, a disruption in the daily routine, so too many people just don't vote. To others, it is an opportunity for gain and advancement, propelling an agenda, or other ends. Whatever the motives, or lack of motives, the bottom line is this, we have a Right and a privilege to choose leaders in this country. Our Right is different than in all other countries in the world, because our election process is still free from the interference of government. Not many nations of the world can claim that. Certainly there is graft and corruption, and the lobbying of special interests that can influence "how" we vote, but the process itself is still relatively the same as our founding fathers intended it long ago.

In the 2018 mid-term election cycle, the democrats made a strong showing, with a fairly high voter turnout. What the party had done very well, was to mobilize their campaigns, with workers and volunteers, that actively encouraged people to vote. Overall, the democrat machine was well tuned, enthusiastic, and passionate, resulting in a good turnout. Despite some of the questionable tactics and methods to get people registered and voted, "the process" of promoting the freedom to vote earns the party a resounding "Kudos"! The exit polling showed a very strong young adult block, but decreased voting from the African-American group, and Hispanic voters.

Mid-aged suburban white women seemed to strongly support the republican candidates, as did increased voters among the Black and Hispanic communities. It is quite likely that many voters were encouraged to vote against the constant maligning of the Kavanaugh appointment, many being former democrats. The greatly improved job situation also prompted minorities to "vote red". The traditional white male voter, backbone of the republican party, actually was down from the 2016 presidential election. Overall, the republicans were weak and pathetic in many races. They were slow and lacking in messaging, showed little passion, and the underlying sentiment was, "who cares". The results were appalling for a party that gained so much just two years earlier when they elected Trump, the Outsider.

The importance of your vote, which is your voice, should be expressed, even now, and especially for the upcoming election. If you can physically do so, do vote. Whether you like a particular candidate or not, or a proposed law that's on a ballot, let your voice be heard. You have the right not to vote, and that is a free decision for you to determine. But not to vote, is surrendering your voice to the outcome of those that did cast their ballots. And, not to vote is essentially voting for the other side.

As our society writhes with turmoil and unrest, forces of change will come about, heading us towards a revolution or major upheaval of our liberties. And at this moment in time, many of these groups will further seek to undermine our rights to vote, our power to voice our opinions, and that would sound the deathblow to America. If our speech (and our choices through voting) are restricted or controlled by laws and deceitful leaders, then the path to a socialistic and then totalitarian country will be complete.

VOTING IS A RIGHT AND PRIVILEGE

Vote, or not, it is your decision, but it far more important than you can imagine. It is your Right, and duty, as a citizen to change the face of the governing bodies, if you so choose. It can not be emphasized enough that the vote is vital in our free society. It is a gift from government, the means to keep control over themselves, a right they both enjoy and despise. With victory, a person can gain power, wealth, and influence. But with defeat, a loss in the power and prestige. Why is it that politicians try to stay in office forever? It is it to serve the needs of the people, or themselves? But it is by the will of the people that leaders are given that privilege. Why do the millions of people want to come to this country? It's not just to shop at Walmart, but to have a free voice in their lives.

The process of voting came about in this country because of the forced hand of the English crown to dictate almost every facet of the lives of the colonial governed. In the new land, the New World, the colonies were largely established to be free of the dictates of their rulers in England. It was often related to spiritual choice and expression, that led groups to the new world seeking some relief from the overlords of government interference with their beliefs and speech, especially when contrary to government actions. The new land meant a certain amount of liberty to express thoughts and ideas, and the election process if not borne, was greatly fostered.

It was greatly due to the interference of the governing bodies in the daily affairs of the colonists, which dissention grew and eventually turned to rebellion, hence the revolution of liberty had come about. Authority over our lives is contrary to our innate sense of freedom and independence.

The founding fathers were absolutely brilliant in their crafting of the constitution, especially in regards to setting up the system of voting. They clearly understood what it meant to have a voice, to be able to freely express an opinion or idea without being arrested or suppressed by those in power. Certainly there are great dissertations of how the system of voting came about, but the point being, it did, and is meant so the common man (now including women) can have some say in how their lives would be governed.

Whether to use your privilege or not, your vote has great influence in every aspect of your life. Elections have consequences. Think about it.

THE CONSTITUTION

Nicely written and clearly defined in the remarkable document, the US Constitution is nothing short of a miraculous template of how to govern a people. Now, one of the chief cornerstones of the constitution, and basic law of the land, is that there are to be periodic elections, free from government interference, for the people to select among themselves the next body of leaders. That is, freely held elections for various offices and levels of government, free from the coercion or compulsion by the government or other persons.

Without this privilege, there is no liberty. It takes time back to the pre-revolutionary days where the government would control what you said, what you did, and all other aspects of life. Without the freedom to choose for ourselves, there is no incentive to improve ones life. Power in the hands of a few elites, has never worked out well for any country, throughout all of human history. What happens in every nation, documented throughout history, is that power corrupts. As power becomes concentrated in the hands of a few, they abuse it. Then the rulers oppress the people. Finally, due to opposition, the rulers mass murder their own citizens to maintain their power. Gratefully, our Founders divided the centers of power, each as a check upon the other.

A people that are free to decide for themselves are happier in their daily lives, more productive, which makes the nation great and prosperous as a whole. That is it in a nutshell, a free people are happier and more productive. And that is the intent of the constitution, individual choice to collectively govern for the good of the whole.

On the federal level, the founding fathers intended that the government's primary role and duty was to provide for the common defense of the nation, and, support the common good. Without defense of the nation, when needed, such as by a foreign invader, then a nation is overrun and destroyed. The Founders understood this all too well in those early times, so in a simplistic but exacting manner, they crafted the document to make provisions for the armed and legal protections for the country. This included, if you study the document, for maintaining and defending the borders. A nation has the sovereign Right to have borders, which is the governments top priority. Without borders, there is no country. Then who decides? The will of the strong, the "rule of the jungle"?

Along with national defense, the Founders tried to instill the idea that if people are left to their own means, they will create jobs and businesses (commerce), for which families and society can provide for their own needs, hence a healthier country. With increased governmental interference in the lives of people, happiness and productivity declines. So the document intended to be in support of the "good works" that people would do, rather than government controlling the daily aspects of life. "The pursuit of happiness" as it reads, means for the government to not interfere with the lives of the people. Laws and rules certainly are needed to govern and maintain the rights and liberties of society, but not into every decision of our personal lives.

Now over two hundred years later, the heavy hand of government has burdened us all with endless regulations, restrictions, and controls, impeding the happiness and contentment of the governed. Rules and laws have restricted many of our rights and liberties the Founders instilled, even to the point of great political controversy. Granted, as our society has changed and developed, a certain amount of governmental control is obviously necessary, but as the government continues to grow, the bureaucracy has strangled many of our rights and privileges, including our freedom of speech, the rights to bear arms, the due process of law, ownership of property, and so on..

THE POLITICAL DIVIDE

Today, right now in America, there are groups that are trying to prevent your freedom of speech to be heard. There are many forces at work to strip away the rights and freedoms we hold, that are sanctioned by our constitutional foundations. Should I name them? They are in every slanderous news and media agency, our teachers and college proessors, half of the current governing body, and the zombie hordes shouting and pillaging as they attempt to suppress contrary thought.

The Zombieists want to divide the people into groups. United we stand, divided we are easily seduced and silenced. We were a nation strongly united in national pride and honor after 911. The differences between parties and peoples were quieter and amicable. Over the past decade or so, the (democrat or socialist) thinking has revolved around division.

Under the Obama/Biden years, they broke the people into groups, and addressed each accordingly. There were republicans, democrats, and independents, as normal, but then groups were further split along demographic and philosophical lines. Blacks and whites, gun owners and anti-gun, pro-life and anti-life, city and rural, conservative and liberal, and every type of group. A speech or event was then twisted by lever words to pit one side against the other, to disrupt actions, and sow discord among each group. Without unity, nothing can get done, unless the government steps in and take control.

Yes, speak out, let your voice be heard with truth or opposing thoughts, but without oppression. That is, if we are adults, let us discuss and reason as adults. When one shouts and fusses, then it is that inner child that needs a "time-out", or maybe a solid spanking. If you don't have anything substantive to offer, then screaming and potty-mouth babble will never sway a debate. For many in our media and leadership roles, they act more like nasty children, than people we should follow or admire.

"When all else fails - scream the race card"

If you disagree with their thinking, these zombie groups will shout you down, or take legal and sometimes violent actions to silence thought. Watching the zombie mobs march down the streets crying and wailing as they throw rocks and destroy property, screaming hateful insults, really does not help their cause. How many news stories and reports have been just that, mob violence. As elections get closer, the divisive rhetoric and violence increases. Is that the new normal for American expression or speech?

It is fair to disagree and oppose the thoughts and ideas of someone else, that is our liberty. If you don't want to listen, that is your right. If you disagree, that is your right. If you want to speak to the contrary and try to persuade others in thinking the same, that is your right also. But is there a line that cannot or should not be crossed? Yes. When you limit and prevent someone else from their rights, that must not happen. Your right is to speak freely, without governmental interference, or other parties suppressing your voice. That is how our fundamental laws work. The rule of law tells us, that "one persons rights end when it interferes with another's".

If there is an alternate or opposing viewpoint on a subject, then "can we not sit down together and reason?" In a society where media and a wide diversity of peoples and opinions abound, there should be great ideas and discussions of every topic and idea to enrich and improve our lives. What we see is the contrary, where the media is controlled by biased deceitful owners and executives (zombie masters), that seek revenues by a ratings ranking systems, hence controlling what the public will view. It is money that drives the media, emotions that fuels the information presented, and the control of free and open speech is the result.

The freedom of speech relates exactly to the freedom and right to vote. If your vote elects leaders that uphold the rule of law, then they are apt to uphold the free dissemination of speech. If you are prevented from voting, intimated, threatened with violence or governmental control, your rights to speak out, through the casting of a vote, is wrong. It is a violation of the most basic of American freedoms, and that must never be allowed to happen.

If poor leaders are elected to office, then they will enact more laws and regulations to limit your freedom of expression, even voting. And what was the basic of all basic American privileges, becomes a memory. With every regulation and law that limits what we can and can not do as a free people, then our liberties disappear. We as a people sink into the historical abyss of government controlling everything, and there is no more freedom. This is also exactly true of every right and freedom guaranteed by our constitution.

SLAVERY IN AMERICA

Throughout human societies, power and control over others is a dark side of our nature. Hence slavery, or the compulsion and control over other people has been a plague not easily cured. America started its young Statehood with slave ownership as a normal part of daily life. Through the struggles of history and blood, the ownership over people had been stopped by constitutional decree. But has it really?

According to studies and reports of world activities on the subject of slavery, there are about 40 nations that practice and allow the ownership of people. America is on that list. The idea of slavery is not just physical ownership, but also through control. Someone who is controlled by another, is that not also slavery, or a form thereof? Control is the drug of the powerful. Throughout history, it was those in power, the rich, the government, the military, and the politicians, that made the rules and laws to control people. Some rules are for the benefit of society as a whole, other regulations are made to increase or hold the power of the elite class. As groups or leaders grow in power, the end result is control. Control leads to restriction, and restriction more often is of rights and liberties, leading to eventual slavery.

Which is which can be determined by the constitution, although the interpretation for modern application becomes debatable. If not stated or with precedence, then a law or ruling may be impeding on our rights. As that pertains to voting, for instance, does that restrict our freedom of speech? What about voter ID laws? Perhaps necessary in the dishonest world we live in, but one can argue that it is a way to restrict that right.

In America today, there are news stories where people are held against their will as slaves (often for personal pleasures), but for the most part, slavery as we define it, is very rare. Not absent in this country, news stories do arise about slavery. It is reasonable to argue that there are other forms of slavery being widely practiced in this country, such as by the banks. If you are in debt, you work as a slave to the bank to try and pay back what is owed. Financial slavery might be considered a type of control over people. Those who struggle with addictions are slaves to that control source. Governmental control by rules and regulations, may not quite be considered slavery, but as more of our rights get stripped away, then we are becoming slaves under legal means.

All of Our Rights are Threatened

Look at the various debates and controversies mentioned today, and ponder whether our rights are being threatened, or society is positively fostered. Are our freedoms and liberties enhanced or preserved as guaranteed by our founding Fathers, or restricted by laws crafted by leaders or groups?

To be bold, look at many of the subjects people talk about. How about marriage and legal relationships? Do laws restrict or enhance "the pursuit of happiness"? If ones actions does not infringe upon another's' right, then constitutionally, maybe it's fine. Do voter laws suppress your right to vote? What would be fair and reasonable to assure "fair and free" elections? Are hate-speech laws lawful? What would constitute "hate", a differing opinion? Too much is being litigated these days because a group or persons finds "offense" or "bad feelings" because of the words of another person. Talk is talk, but when it comes to laws, that sounds more like the suppression of free speech.

How about gun laws and restricting the Right to bear arms? The intent of the Founders was to assure that the people would be able to defend themselves and their families from harm, and, to oppose a government that was unjust (tyrannical according to the document). Any infringement made by government is a violation of our rights. Don't accept the lies argued to the contrary. The Bill of Rights has this as the number two in importance for a reason, it's important.

Here also, religious teachings are also in the center of controversy these days. Speech and religion are the first and most important rights the founders declared. Why, that was what the English rulers suppressed most. You must not restrict free thought or personal preference of spiritual worship. That also includes the fight over abortion. What is life, the handling of "the pursuit of happiness" in conflict with religious belief, speech, and law? Laws are words spoken by men. Some are for the good of the nation and its citizens, others are for power and gain. When government enacts laws to restrict either speech or religion, that is wrong.

Important to note, there are great lengths happening right now in this country to control these rights, and that spells the end of American liberty, and ushers in the destruction of this nation. Watch and glean from every news story, every speech made, every law and action taken, to see if our freedoms are being upheld or restricted.

No Tolerance for (Christian) Religious Thought

The same is true about ones spiritual worship. America is a land for anyone to worship freely as they so choose. Freedom of religion is essentially the second half of the First Amendment. But speak the name of Jesus Christ, and can you face persecution, punishment, fines, and possibly imprisonment. The same people that cry for tolerance, are the ones that shout insults and intolerance when mentioning anything Christian or biblically related.

Prior to 1960, the Bible was freely taught in public schools, prayer was practiced, and nativity scenes marked the Christmas holiday season. After 1960, Bible teaching was ousted from public schools, prayer was later banished, and not long after that, the radicals took Christ out of Christmas. In 1980, the Supreme court voted to ban the Ten Commandments from being displayed in public buildings, like courthouses and schools. Is the freedom to worship, or at least the Christian faith, banned from the public view?

The radical cite Jefferson's thinking that government should be separate from religion, the "Separation of Church and State" thinking. But hear too, the radicals got it twisted around, a clear attempt to get God out of our lives. No, Jefferson was concerned that government should not instill a state-mandated religion, like the English crown did over the American colonials. Not the separation of church from State, but rather the interference of government in our religious choices. America is founded upon Christian-Judeo values, namely the Bible. Our laws and system of justice is all biblically based. Most of the Founding Father's were strong faith-filled Christian men, as were (and still many are) members at all levels of government. It is not that being of one faith is right or wrong, especially to be a believer working as a public servant, but being a person of faith in public service instills a sense of duty to serve the people.

But to incite any other religion into the public square, it brings praises of "tolerance" and "inclusiveness" by the social warriors. And then to shove down the throats of our children in public school, that Christmas is about everybody and everything (expect Christ), is a violation of the 1st Amendment. And God forbid our children from reading the Ten Commandments. They might actually obey them.

GUN CONTROL – A RIGHT UNDER SIEGE

More gun control? With every shooting, police involvement or not, the anti-gun activists clamor for more controls, and getting rid of the second amendment. There are some 140 million gun owners in this country, and to threaten government seizure our weapons may be the spark to an all-out civil war, From law enforcement to ex-military, and the common man, having guns is vital for personal defense, and the protection of private property. The ideas of rights, and the unlawful seizures and further restrictions cuts right to the core of government taking away our rights, which should be resisted.

And with every publicized incidence, politicians come up with a myriad of crazy solutions, but continue to ignore the problem. There are plenty of gun laws on the books, good ones, but they are not fully enforced. Add a thousand more laws and regulations, yet it will do nothing more than keep good honest citizens from legally being able to protect themselves. also, more insane regulations and restrictions will further incite more illegal gun violence. On the other hand, criminals and illegal aliens are armed with all sorts of firearms, laws or not. A criminal will have all of the guns and bad stuff they want, laws or not. If criminals are able to have guns, but the regular honest person are not, then this too is a powder keg that could ignite the next civil war. It seems that the laws protect the criminals, but the honest folks are forced to prove their innocence.

Is it not so? Last year in Richmond, Virginia, there was to be a pro-gun, pro-family, pro-American rally. The rally was well promoted to the governor and the press about how regular people need to protect themselves and support for the laws. The governor, the media, and various anti-American groups all opposed the proposed rally, calling for police barricades and threatening bringing in the national guard, fearing that a gathering would be a hot-spot for "white supremacist" groups. Yet, this same (democrat) governor did nothing to stop the riots and violence that happened in Charlottesville.

If a conservative group, like those supporting pro-life, or pro-constitutional rights tries to have a march, then the (democrat) leaders, the media, and anti-American groups, opposes them. It is very clear, that when a riot happens, these same groups and leaders sing their praises and do nothing to support our rights or protect the people. Why is it upside down? And again, do the research yourself, and you will find, that it is the democrat leaders, mayors, city council members, and governors, that oppose the rights of people in favor of mob rule.

It is telling that the media and the politicians don't as much greave with the victims, as President Trump does, but instead they just cry out for more controls and gun confiscation. This was again the case with the George Floyd death in Minneapolis, and with the shooting death in Atlanta, shortly thereafter. The media, and these rioters care more about their anti-police, anti-gun bias, than they mourn for the victims. This facade by these leftwing people is very clear, which furthers the divide in this country.

These same clamorous groups demand intensive Universal Background Checks, limits on magazine size, eliminating certain types of weapons from the marketplace. These are the typical knee-jerk emotional reactions tat come about every time. There is increased talk about gun confiscation, often citing countries like Australia, and how it has "worked" there. Are these the answers? No! "Guns don't kill people, people kill people." Gun restricting laws do not save lives, but actually puts more people at risk. Restrict the good and regular law-abiding citizen from protecting themselves, and only the criminals and government will have guns. Does that make us safer?

In America, certain areas have high crime rates, other areas are less so, and the loss of life must never be down played. Life is precious, everyone's, not just one group or another, but everybody. All the laws in the world can never end gun violence. Why? Because criminals don't obey laws, it is that simple. Honest citizens follow the law, and adding more gun laws just hurts everyone. The bigger picture is simply this, the federal government does Not have the constitutional right to restrict or regulate our firearms. Yet, our rights as private citizens are greatly restricted by many federal laws. If the founding Fathers could only see how much we have shredded our county's establishment, they would call for another revolution. These are perilous times, and sadly, with every disastrous or tragic event, "We the People" eagerly surrender more and more of our freedoms to the mob rule, and to the central government.

The 2nd Amendment reads: "A well regulated Militia, being necessary to the security of a free State, the right of the people to keep and bear Arms, shall not be infringed".

What that means is that the feds are to "piss off" (according to one commentator), regarding any regulation of our firearms. Study the history and the intent of the founding Fathers when they wrote the Bill of Rights. They had a great document for establishing the new country, but they felt something more was needed to define individual Rights that the federal government should not touch. Everything else not specifically stated was to be relegated to the States.

The whole point of the revolution was that the central government was unjust and "tyrannical" in the abuse of governing powers towards the citizens. It was only because the citizens had arms, and took up arms, to defy the government, that there was a revolt. Without the governed having their firearms, the government would have simply used their armaments and force to squash any opposition. In fact, they tried, but the people fought back.

The government, the federal government at least, is not to limit or restrict this right. It is most closely related to the 1st Amendment of free speech, because the people have the right to speak out against the government, and to assemble (peacefully). Also the 2nd is closely associated with the 4th and 5th, as the people have the rights to own property and not be subject to search and seizure without due process. The more you read and learn about those early days of the nation, it was so important to spell out what the government did not have control over.

What about Abortion? A Right or Wrong?

The Zombieists and their hordes, that are trying to change America, wanting to take away individual rights and freedoms, are the same ones that enact laws to kill babies. On the one hand they call for saving illegal alien children at the border, but turn around and enact laws to kill our own citizens.

Again, they play the double-standard, and profess needing equality and fairness for all. Yes, there is an epidemic of gun-related deaths, but what about abortion? If a criminal with a gun attacks you, and you do not have one, then you become an innocent victim. What about a baby, the most precious and innocent of all life, murdered in cold blood, under the guise of legality? Which is worse, or what's the difference? In America, you have the Constitutional Right to defend yourself, even with a gun. But who defends a baby?

The recent New York State abortion law, essentially sanctions death to their citizens. Human babies can be killed late in the pregnancy, and even after the baby is born and takes its first breaths. This became law also in Virginia, with the approval of the democrat governor that has demonstrated how he supports chaos versus law and order. This same governor has been caught on video in bad behavior, but media and his party chooses to turn a "blind eye". There is something very wrong when our elected leaders usurp the common morality and traditions of the nation, and dishonor the oath of office they have taken.

Up until now, every statute in this country would call these late-term abortions as murder! Not anymore. This is a violation of our Rights of Worship, Speech, and the pursuit of happiness, and other guarantees as laid out in the constitution. Other states like Vermont and California has wanted similar laws. The deceptive politicians and some within the legal establishment will profess the contrary, but they are vicious liars and murderers.

We are a nation of laws, and the rule of law is the intent of how our leaders are suppose to govern our society. But laws are made that are not always good or right for the people. All abortion laws are legal, but none of them are right. It is by the twisting and perversion of right and wrong by filthy lawyers and crooked politicians that has brought us to this point. It is time to act and do something.

The majority of these politicians are democrats, but includes weak limp-wristed republicans also. Look at the voting records, it is very telling. These are the same hypocrites that cry out about the injustices of handling illegal alien children being held by border control officers, or those crying to "save the planet". But when it comes to killing human babies, our own citizens, these people and the media remain silent. They have traded their morale compass for humanistic ideals?

Do you think these elected officials care about your gun rights, your freedom to worship, or to speak against evil? Do you think they are upholding the statutes of the constitution? Whatever the issue, gun laws, rights of life, illegals crossing into our country, what is happening is the shredding of the foundational principles and protections laid out in the constitution. The more they create new laws, the closer America will become like Nazi Germany.

And what about a child's "the right to life"? The abortion question, is not just a freedom of religious worship, but it is also a freedom of speech. Perhaps the greater overall question is whether it is right and lawful for the government to kill, or sanction the killing, of its own citizens. Although the Supreme Court allowed the ability to kill unborn babies as a rule of law in Roe vs. Wade, is it right? No, it is a disgusting and abhorrence to everything good and honorable that this country touts to be. Murder is murder. An unborn child is still a human being, up until now. How can these wise lawyers in the Supreme Court, who are charged in upholding the constitution, allow such debauchery? Because liberal presidents appointed liberal-thinking justices into the court, so poor laws get enacted and enforced. They care nothing about the Rule of Constitutional Law, but instead focus on the emotional political fad of the day. America is heading down the road to destruction if this trend continues.

When the States of New York and Virginia passed the new laws allowing the death of babies, the voting assembly members applauded the new laws with resounding glee! It is said that liberty will die with resounding applause. Soon, more states will enact laws contrary to tradition and justice. That is sounding more like Nazi Germany, the Soviet Union, or China. Are we really there?

Whether life begins at conception or when a baby draws its first breath is irrelevant. The question is how can we as a nation allow the murder of our own innocent and defenseless citizens? We are suppose to be a nation ruled by law, but not all laws are good or just. Where is the sanity of our lawmakers? This is murder, plain and simple. We need to act.

Elections have consequences. You vote for good people to lead us, that defend life and liberty, or not. We have seen the definitions of right or wrong changed to suit the desires of the mob, and by elected officials. You vote for your hearts desire, and apparently it's for death. And to have such leaders in power, they will continue to enact laws that will subvert and limit more of our rights.

Now if this horrid lust of killing innocent life is not overruled, then the rights of free speech, religious worship, and "the pursuit of happiness", are made mute. Our freedoms as guaranteed under the US Constitution will be destroyed. Those lawmakers, supporters of such legislation, and any group or organizations that adheres with such, are murders and co-conspirators. Then if this persists, then truth and justice in America is a lie!

What follows next? Well, because the murder of babies is made legal, the next step is to broaden that "definition" of whom can be (legally) murdered. Next will be young children no longer wanted by their parents, or perhaps the elderly will be killed at the whim of a politician. Then from there, any opposition group or segment of citizens, like white males, Christians, deplorable Trump supporters, and so on, can face the death squads (by law). "When the sword is unsheathed, it is difficult to put it back without first spilling blood."

ABOUT LOSING OUR LIBERTIES

The point of this book is to alert and remind ourselves that we are a nation of laws, and that we as citizens have rights and freedoms guaranteed to us by our founding document, the Constitution. Rather than get into the "nuts and bolts" of the laws and proposed ideas of what and how new and old regulations work, my intent is to suggest that our "inalienable rights" are being squashed. Is it possible to lose our Constitutional rights and freedoms? These are guaranteed under the law, aren't they? Yes, but No.

With each election, the results are more radical-thinking politicians taking office, by which they get laws and regulations passed to silence free speech, and other rights. Not so long ago, one could talk openly of another person or a group of people, have heated opposing debate, but that now is limited by "hate speech laws" and other controls. Yes, for sure it is not nice or kind to talk ill of another person or group, but can we not speak what's on our mind anymore? What if you spoke against a government agency or a governmental employee? Laws are being passed to limit what you can say against the government. What was accountability of government by the people, laws are starting to restrict that opposition, and then bring about serious consequences. The silencing of open discussion, debate, or defiance, is control of our liberty. Some politicians seek more control over us by enacting more laws and regulations in every area of our lives. Learn who the candidates are before you vote. Does the party platform, their set of ideals, align with your own, and how you want to live? Do the candidates or leaders act to enhance the people of the nation, or are they grabbing power and influence?

If democrat politicians (who have the mission to control the lives of the people) are elected, they will enact laws to reduce or eliminate the rights and privileges we hold. This is the trend we have been witnessing over the past decade at least. In particular, our freedom to speak in opposition, our rights to bear arms, and so on. As we lose our freedom of speech (again as an example), we become slaves to the government. And from slavery, comes the destruction of the nation.

Don't the republicans seek control also? Yes, sure they do, as all that are elected are subject to the lusts of power and control. It's just that in recent times, the democrat party has become so radical in their quest to control people by restrictive laws and regulations. Is that right or even fair? Some think it's fine, others are less happy, but the movement towards a socialist and totalitarian slavery will end the liberties and freedoms we still have. This trend in our recent elections, with the types of people elected is actually very scary. Too many are pushing for a government-led, governmental-controlled society. All countries that have embraced that style of slavery, are unproductive, with a people that are unhappy. Those nations, historically, have not remained very long.

"Those who gain power will abuse it, and then they will oppress the people, which then they will start murdering the citizenry." Strongly ponder these thoughts, it happened throughout history.

MAKE A DIFFERENCE

Your vote does count. Your vote is your voice. It's a liberty and a right that must not be silenced or impeded by opposition, or by the government. To allow your voice to be shut down, you lose the one easy, and best, freedom a citizen can hold. "Use it or lose it", is a cliche sometimes used, and it is applicable now. Voting is your decision, take a stand, either "for" or "against", but voice your opinion, it does matter.

Our government was founded on the principle that if people are left to live their lives freely, society grows and prospers, supported by happy citizens. Creativity and invention, improvements of life, make for a better world. As simplistic as that sounds, basically it's true. Our system of government was designed and set up to assure the people would have the liberty to become all they can aspire to do. The freedom of free and open speech has been the cornerstone of the greatness this country has shared, rooted in the process of free and open elections. Every vote counts, and every citizen has a duty to make this country better, according to their own conscience.

The importance of your vote, which is your voice, should be expressed, even now, and especially for this upcoming election. If you can physically do so, do vote. As mentioned previously, whether you like a particular party or candidate, or a person seeking reelection, let your voice be heard. You right is also not to vote, which is your free decision. But , is surrendering your voice by not voting, is to submit to the will of someone else.

As our society writhes with turmoil and unrest, forces of change come about, heading towards a revolution or major upheaval of our liberties. And in this country, at this moment in time, many people and groups, seek to undermine our rights to vote, our power of speech, all of our other freedoms and liberties we still have. That would sound the death-blow to America.

ABOUT THE AUTHOR

I grew up in a middle class family, had a father that worked, a mother that stayed home and raised children, the typical traditional American home. We had a small house, one car, (no) white picket fence, we had pets, regular schooling, church-goers, watched news and various TV shows, and had all of the cliche normal things in life typified during the 1950s and 60s. Life was normal and decent, reasonably peaceful, and safe.

My father was a veteran, worked a blue collar job, and was a straight-line democrat, just like his father before him. The Kennedy era thinking of party politics was pretty much his thinking as well. And for many decades, that seemed to work well in America. I too learned and adopted similar ideas of how life and government should work and coexist.

But that has changed radically over the past couple decades as the democrat party is no longer the party of the average working man. One would best describe the party as what we used to call the Communist-Socialist party during that earlier era. Now the party is all about hate speech, bigotry, division, dirty-politics, rampant dishonesty and deception by party leaders and candidates, and everything revolving around government control. This is no longer the democrat party America once loved.

The candidates and false narratives they promoted were enough to make me switch parties. Over the last many election cycles while the democrats drove further left, I pushed my family and friends to switch parties and vote further right. Not that the republicans are perfect by any means, but they do hold to more of the values and principles I do. The biggest area where they align with my own thinking are the ideas of limited government, a government hands-off ideology, and support of the Constitution and the foundations of this country. Upholding our rights and freedoms are more their forte, so this is where we will stay.

My hope is to share these thoughts with you, so that you can glean some insight of the struggle we face over our dying liberties. Thank you reading this.

Also consider these other books written about our Rights and Freedoms. These also are found on Amazon Kindle under the Politics section. Look for:

The American Civil War II
By T. H. Logwood
ASIN: B08CQ4PDMQ.

* * * * *

Don't Tread on Me
By T. H. Logwood
ASIN: B07X5DRRYB

* * * * *

I Met a Man Named Donald
By T. H. Logwood
ASIN: B0842YF1HH.

* * * * *

"The End of American Liberty"
by T. H. Logwood
ASIN: B07HPYZWTF

* * * * *

Repent America, In the Name of Jesus!

By T. H. Logwood
ASIN: B07NBXYLLB

* * * * *

"The Democrat Blue Wave is the Texas 2nd Alamo"
by T. H. Logwood
ASIN: B07N7N2WG6

* * * * *

"The End of American Freedom"
by T. H. Logwood
ASIN: B07MSJ4QD7

* * * * *

"The U.S.S. La Porte (APA 151), The Pearl of the Pacific"
by T. H. Logwood
ASIN: B07L6JXRB9

* * * * *

"A Walk in the Sub-Alpine Meadows: A Look at the Tuoloume Meadows Ecosystem"
by T. H. Logwood
ASIN: B07HM928TH

* * * * *

"Collecting Old Stock Certificates: A Look at the Past"
by T. H. Logwood
ASIN: B07HNX1FGK

www.ingramcontent.com/pod-product-compliance
Lightning Source LLC
Chambersburg PA
CBHW051123250726
48655CB00007B/2846